THE WRITE RULES

TECHNICAL WRITING/PRESENTATION AND ENGLISH AS A SECOND LANGUAGE GUIDE

JOAN RAMIREZ

Disclaimer: This handbook is intended to help individuals in Engineering and Technical industries and English as Second Language professionals enhance their client rosters. Its contents are not a guarantee of same.

Only perseverance can accomplish that task. So study and write on.

Copyright 2020 by JL Regen Enterprises

All rights reserved.

No part of this book may be reproduced, photocopied, stored in a retrieval system, or transmitted electronically without the author's prior permission.

Cover design by: Karen Phillips

PRINT ISBN: 978-0-9984099-3-1

EBOOK ISBN: 978-0-9984099-4-8

CONTENTS

Foreword	vii
1. USING THE WRITING RULES PROPERLY	1
PARTS OF SPEECH	1
THE DETERMINERS	4
COMMON GRAMMAR MISTAKES	5
PUNCTUATION	7
2. COMMON WRITING ERRORS	11
SIMPLIFY TERMS, WORDS, AND SENTENCES	11
WATCH VERBS AND HOW THEY WORK	13
COMPARISON OF ADVERBS AND ADJECTIVES	14
AVOID NEEDLESS REPETITION	15
USE ACTIVE VOICE	17
3. BUSINESS WRITING	19
HOW TO WRITE CLEAR, CONCISE, EFFECTIVE BUSINESS EMAILS	19
WRITING EXERCISES	21
Sample Letters Used in Business Correspondence	22
HOW TO WRITE INTERNET ARTICLES THAT WILL ATTRACT CLIENTS	25
4. PRESENTATIONS	29
HOW TO WRITE A SPEECH	29
HOW TO GIVE A PRESENTATION: VERBAL AND POSTURE TIPS	30
5. COMMUNICATION	33
HOW LISTENING SKILLS CAN HELP YOU ACHIEVE YOUR GOALS	33
HOW TO DEVELOP TELEPHONE LISTENING SKILLS	34
6. ENGLISH AS A SECOND LANGUAGE (ESL) TIPS	37
CORRECT WORD USAGE	37
NOTING DESCRIPTIONS	40

7. PROMOTING YOUR BUSINESS	43
MARKETING TECHNIQUES FOR EMERGING BUSINESS OWNERS	43
ORGANIZATIONS TO PROMOTE YOUR BUSINESS	46
8. Writing Resources	57
Wrap Up	59
Acknowledgments	61
About the Author	63

IT'S NEVER TOO EARLY OR LATE TO FULFILL YOUR DESTINY. My writing handbook, for Engineering, Technical, and English as Second Language professionals, will enhance your written and verbal communications skill set. After reading this book and using the examples, you will be able to attract and retain clients. The concise but effective guidelines in the handbook will ensure your business grows to its full potential. However, you will have to work hard to achieve your goals. Success, unlike oatmeal, isn't instant!

"This book gives clear writing guidelines—keep it concise and simple." — Kelly, PE

"Joan has compiled a fine communications guide. If you're looking for a concise reference to help you with your verbal and written communication skills, The Write Rules is for you." — Steven, French teacher

FOREWORD

With the passage of time the population of engineers for whom English is a second language has increased to the point where they exceed the native English speakers. This has created a situation where it has become difficult for these individuals to express themselves. Therefore, additional training and reading is required to increase their proficiency with the English language—written and spoken. An engineer who can't communicate his or her findings to a client is ineffective.

I hope this book will help to ameliorate this situation.

Ivan Ramirez, BE, MS, Licensed Professional Engineer- NY and NJ, Certified Building Inspection Engineer

Chapter One
USING THE WRITING RULES PROPERLY

PARTS OF SPEECH

Nouns (naming words) – Nouns come in abstract and concrete forms. They are the most common part of speech.

An abstract – home
A concrete – house
A person – teacher
A specific person – Maggie
A place – city
A specific place – New York City
A thing – television, shirt, chair
An idea – happiness, sadness, peace
A quality – bravery

1. **New York City** is my **home**.
2. **Robert** evaluated the **chair**.
3. **Frances** believes in **peace**.
4. The **report** is ready for distribution.

Pronouns - replaces a noun to make sentences shorter and clearer
A person – he, her
A group of people – they, them
A thing or a place – it

1. **He** lives in New York City
2. **They** vacationed at the beach.
3. **It** stopped working last night.

Adjectives – describes a noun, limits a noun. It is a modifier of a noun or pronoun. Adjectives make the meaning of a noun more precise
A person – big, small, brave, honest
A place – large, beautiful, busy, complex
A thing – heavy, light, colorful

Any of the adjectives used as examples above could be used with any nouns or pronouns.

1. I don't like **loud** music because it gives me an earache.
2. **Honest** Mark can always be counted on to get the job done.
3. **Yellow** paint is required for the warning sign.

Verbs – State an action, an occurrence, or a state of being. Without a verb, you cannot make a sentence.
Action – walk, play, go, come, do

Occurrence – happen, became
State of being – be, is, are, feel

1. **Turn** left at the signal.
2. After passing the exam, he **became** a certified engineer.
3. Joe and Sam **are** business partners.
4. Cyd **hates** to eat alone.

Adverbs - Describe, limit an adjective, a verb, or another adverb. Adverbs make language more precise by describing how something happens.

When? – Joseph **always** arrives early to work.

How? – Carolyn manages her team **well**.

In what way? – He is talking **slowly** so she can understand what he's saying

To what extent? – He performed the work **rapidly**.

Be careful not to overuse adverbs.

Prepositions - Are words that relate words to each other in a phrase or sentence. Prepositions show the relationship between a noun or a pronoun with another word in the sentence.
Typical examples: in, on, under, over, at, to, by, off

1. He sat **on** the chair
2. Freda found the eraser **in** the cup **on** the desk.
3. She drove **over** the bridge.

4. Badu found the missing watch **at** the beach.
5. The book belongs **to** Mark.
6. The loud noise came **from within** the stadium. (double preposition)

Conjunctions – Words that connect parts of a sentence. They connect words or groups of words.

Common conjunctions are: And, But, Or, So

1. I tried to hit the nail, **but** hit my thumb instead.
2. Jessie bought a bike **for** commuting to work.
3. You can have watermelon **or** peaches.
4. My mother always worked two jobs **so** we could afford the things we needed for school.

THE DETERMINERS

Articles

"a" and "an" are general
"the" is specific

1. Robert has **a** book in his hand. (Use "a" before a consonant "b" sound.)
2. **An** apple a day keeps the doctor away. (Use "an" before a vowel "a" sound.)
3. I want **the** computer I saw in the window.

Possessive (your, his, her, my, their, our)

1. I want **your** vote to count in the next election.
2. **His** shoelaces are always untied.
3. My mother gave me a lot of **her** advice when I was a child.

4. **Their** unit will be shipping out next month.
5. Our only hope of escape is through **her** window.

COMMON GRAMMAR MISTAKES

Noun-Verb Agreement

Wrong: Writing and speaking is two important forms of communication.

Correct: Writing and speaking are two important forms of communication.

Explanation: There are two nouns—writing and speaking—so you need the plural verb "are."

Sentence Fragment

Wrong: Marcus has arrived. In the house.

Correct: Marcus has arrived in the house.

Explanation: You need to complete the action of Marcus to show he is in the house.

Run-on Sentence

Wrong: You know what a dictionary is. It has a lot of definitions.

Correct: You know that a dictionary has a lot of definitions of words.

Explanation: A run-on sentence is a disconnect in a complete thought. Combine them to make one sentence that expresses what you want to say.

Misused Article

Wrong: He called **a** hour ago

Correct: He called **an** hour ago.

Correct: He said to call an hour (**H** here is a soft sound—don't pronounce it) before midnight.

Correct: I have decided to write a paper (**P** is a hard consonant—pronounce it) on hurricanes.

Explanation: When you have a consonant "h" that has a soft sound, you must use the article "an."
"A" is used before words starting in hard consonant sounds (sounds that you can hear) and "an" is used before words starting with vowel and vowel-like sounds: a, e, i, o, u. NOTE: "h" has a vowel-like sound.

Possessive Use

Wrong: Ricks editor didn't like his article.

Correct: Rick's editor didn't like his article.

Explanation: When you have a possessive, you must use the apostrophe (')

Split Infinitive

Wrong: I decided to regularly use my calculator to balance my checkbook.

Correct: I decided <u>to use</u> my calculator on a regular basis to balance my checkbook.

Explanation: Infinitives go together. Don't split them.

NEVER USE: To regularly buy
ALWAYS USE: To buy on a regular basis or To buy regularly

PUNCTUATION
Commas

Use commas between proper names and titles.

The German writer, Hermann Hesse, is a favorite with college students.

Use commas to separate parts of an address.

1. The Director comes from Chicago, Illinois and now lives in London, England.
2. The fire started at Joe's Clam House, 1923 Seventh Street, Los Angeles, California and spread throughout the neighborhood.
3. I live on Mulberry Street in downtown Atlanta, Georgia.

Use commas to separate items.

The colors were red, white, and blue; green, white, and orange; and red, yellow, and gray.

NOTE THE ABOVE SENTENCE: You need semicolons due to internal punctuation with a series.
   If this isn't clear, take the sentence apart:
   red, white, and blue;
   green, white, and orange;
   red, yellow, and gray

Use commas after introductory terms that express time.

Examples:

1. Yesterday, I flew to Paris and had dinner at a charming bistro.
2. Today, I am going to finish the project.
3. Tomorrow, I am going to apply for a driver's license. (Note the apostrophe with the possessive.)

Periods

A sentence within a sentence is punctuated according to the needs of the longer sentence.

. . .

Example: "I'll pass this exam," she said (but was not really certain that she would).

Quote Marks

If a sentence contains a quotation, the comma goes INSIDE the closing quotation mark.

Examples:
"To be or not to be," Hamlet stated.
"You are a fool to think he didn't rob the bank," the manager said.

Terms of Reference
p.=page
pp.=pages

Apostrophe

One person: The sales representative's commission

Plural: Those are the technicians' tools.

> DO NOT use IT's when you mean ITS
> IT'S = IT IS

Chapter Two
COMMON WRITING ERRORS

SIMPLIFY TERMS, WORDS, AND SENTENCES

Use Simpler Terms

Wrong: If we don't expound in terminology everyone comprehends, there will be massive miscommunication.

Correct: We should explain in clear English so everyone will understand.

Explanation: Don't get fancy when trying to convey a message. Write in clear, concise terms.

Repeated Words

Wrong: Who can forget Springtime Paris when the weather changes in the spring?

Correct: Who can forget Paris in spring weather?

Explanation: Don't repeat words that mean the same thing: springtime=spring.

Also, use lower case for spring.

Don't Split The Pairs

Wrong: The shipment will EITHER arrive on Monday OR Wednesday.

Correct: The shipment will arrive EITHER on Monday OR Wednesday.

Explanation: Do not split Either/Or and Neither/Nor phrases.

Never End a Sentence with a Preposition

Wrong: The man whom I spoke with wasn't the one I had been referred to.

Correct: The man I spoke to wasn't the one to whom I was referred.

Never Repeat Words

Wrong: The unit contains 232 units.

Correct: The facility contains 232 units.

Never Use Double Negatives

>**Wrong:** The engine had hardly no systemic care.

>**Correct:** The engine had only a little systemic care.

WATCH VERBS AND HOW THEY WORK
Always Use Active Verbs

>**Wrong:** The agreement was broken by the partners.

>**Correct:** The partners broke the agreement.

Subject and Verb Tenses Must Always Agree

>**Wrong:** The solution are easy.

>**Correct:** The solutions are easy.

Never Switch Verb Tenses

>**Wrong:** I was at home because I am sick.

>**Correct:** I was home because I was sick.

Do Not Make Verbs Out of Nouns

Wrong: He detailed the negative aspects of the speech.

Explanation: *Detail* is a noun

Correct: He explained the negative aspects of the speech.

Do Not Use an Adjective as an Adverb

Wrong: This computer obsoletes all others.

Correct: This computer is obsolete.

COMPARISON OF ADVERBS AND ADJECTIVES

POSITIVE	COMPARATIVE	SUPERLATIVE
strong	stronger	strongest
fair	fairer	fairest
bad	worse	worst
good	better	best
little	less	least
some	more	most

For example:
1. Wilson is the best of the lot.
2. Ben is the fastest runner on the team.

NEVER SAY: John acted caringly.
READ OUT LOUD TO SEE IF IT MAKES SENSE.

SAY: John acted in haste.
SAY: John acted with care.

GOOD and WELL
Good is always an adjective.
Well is always an adverb.

Examples:
1. He is a good student.
2. He works well.

VERY
Don't use this unless it is a serious situation.

Examples:

1. I am very sorry for your loss.
2. I am very concerned about my son's grades.

AVOID NEEDLESS REPETITION

Wrong: The provision of Section 5 provides for a union shop.
Correct: Section 5 provides for a union shop.

Wrong: The assignment of training the ineffective worker is an assignment we must carry out.
Correct: Training the ineffective worker is a crucial assignment.

Wrong: In my opinion I think that the plan is sound.
Correct: The plan is sound.

Wrong: He reported for work on Friday morning at eight o'clock in the morning.
Correct: He reported for work at eight o'clock in the morning.

RULE: WRITE OUT NUMBERS FROM ONE TO NINE.

There were five grids to analyze.

She found nine errors in the document.

The equipment passed the test 58 times.

The car traveled 345 miles on one tank of gas.

Don't Clutter Your Writing

DON'T USE	DO USE
For the purpose of	For
In the near future	Soon
In accordance with	By
In view of the fact that	Since, Because
On the occasion of	On
Is of the opinion	Believes
Involved in the task	Reviewing
It is the committee's assumption	Assumes
At the present time	Now
Due to the fact that	Due to, Because
Impacted	Affected
It is recommended that	I, We recommend
On the grounds that	Because, Since
Provided that	If
Until such time as	Until
It is requested that	Please

Examples:

Wrong: For the purpose of this report, it is requested that you provide feedback within 30 days.
Correct: For this report, please provide feedback within 30 days.

Wrong: The blue team is of the opinion that the upgrades are necessary
Correct: The blue team believes that the upgrades are necessary.

USE ACTIVE VOICE

Keep Your Correspondence in the Active Voice by Using Subject/Noun

Wrong: The agreement was broken by the partners.
Correct: The partners **broke** the agreement.

Wrong: A need exists for a greater candidate selection efficiency.
Correct: We must **select** candidates more efficiently.

Wrong: It has come to my attention that you are using the wrong cartridge.
Correct: I **suggest** you check the printer cartridge.

BUSINESS WRITING

HOW TO WRITE CLEAR, CONCISE, EFFECTIVE BUSINESS EMAILS

STEP ONE – Create a Draft That Includes the Important Information

WHO—individuals on your project team

WHAT—project name and description

WHY-reasons for the project and your involvement

WHEN –timeframe for completion

WHERE—location(s) and contacts with emails and phone numbers

HOW—procedures to follow

STEP TWO – Enter the Appropriate Descriptive Data

I like to use this one to start every email. If you have one that fits your needs, please use it.

SAMPLE
    DATE:
    TO:
    FROM:
    SUBJECT: (Title of the Project)

STEP THREE – Compose the body of the email
    (Note the three bullets below headings—Be brief. You can always expand on this in a meeting.)

WHAT IS THE OBJECTIVE?

WHAT ARE THE DISADVANTAGES?
-
-

WHAT ARE THE ADVANTAGES?
-
-

WHAT ARE YOUR RECOMMENDATIONS? This can be tricky. If you're the Project Manager, take the lead. If you're part of a team, please ask for every member's input.

WRITING EXERCISES

Responding to an Unhappy Customer

Before looking at the AFTER example, beyond the centered straight-line break, REWRITE the following letter without the clutter. Give yourself a bonus point for clutter phrases not found in the Don't Clutter Your Writing list.

BEFORE:

Dear Mr. Delano:

It has come to our attention that you are not happy with the service that you have come to expect with regards to your new refrigerator.

We at All-Dell Appliances are of the opinion that you are deserving of a replacement. It is indeed unfortunate due to the fact that the model you selected was out of stock, you chose one that wasn't a good fit for your kitchen.

May you let us know when we can call you at the number of your choice to arrange for pickup of said refrigerator? It goes without saying we will refund the money to your credit card and are ready to help you pick out a new one.
We at All-Dell Appliances value your business and look forward to serving you in the near future with all of your kitchen needs.

Very truly,
Fred Astrange
908-907-0978
fredastrang@all-dellappliances.com

AFTER:

Dear Mr. Delano:

I am sorry that you're not pleased with your new refrigerator.

<u>*(YOU ARE RESPONSIBLE. YOU ARE THE MANAGER).*</u>

You deserve the best. On behalf of the store, I want you to be happy with your purchase. When can I call you to arrange for pickup of the item and assist you in ordering a replacement?

<u>*(THIS SHOWS YOU CARE AND HOPEFULLY, WILL RESULT IN A FINAL SALE).*</u>

I and All-Dell Appliances value your business and look forward to accommodating your kitchen needs.

Very truly,
Fred Astrange
Client Services Manager/All-Dell Appliances
908-907-0978
fredastrang@all-dellappliances.com

SAMPLE LETTERS USED IN BUSINESS CORRESPONDENCE

Thank You Follow Up Email for New Business Lead

Dear Mr. Jenson:

It was a pleasure speaking with you today. The decision is yours to make, but I do hope that you will consider Chandler Construction.

I'm attaching a list of our services for your reference.

Please don't hesitate to contact me regarding areas that I might not have covered in our conversation.

Very truly,

Raymond Chandler
President
Chandler Construction
raycc@gmail.com
203-456-9087

Close A Business Deal

Dear Mr. Essex:

I'm delighted you have chosen Samuelson Ltd. for your electrical needs.

I've attached a contract for your review and signature.

I'm forwarding your name, email, and phone number to our Project Manager for new building installations.
Please contact him with any additional questions.

Very truly,

Edward Practer
Vice President for Business Development
eprac@samuelsonltd.com
212-897-6098
cc: Albert Gonzalez, Installation Manager
agonzalez@samuelsonltd.com
212-897-6099

CAUSE and EFFECT
　One action (cause) taken in good faith has a positive result (effect).
　OR
　One action (cause) taken in good faith has a negative result (effect).

ADVICE: ALWAYS THINK OF THE CONSEQUENCES OF YOUR ACTIONS.

THINK OF THE EFFECT OF YOUR DECISION.

Exercise 1

Use each of the following words in a sentence. Assume the reader's native language isn't English. Be clear and concise.
　Profit
　Revenue
　Recession
　Friction
　Valve
　Incinerator

TO SELF CORRECT:

LOOK AT THE EXAMPLES IN THE DICTIONARY AND MAKE 100% SURE YOU'VE USED EACH WORD <u>CORRECTLY</u>.

PLEASE PROOFREAD YOUR WORK AND SPELL <u>CORRECTLY</u>.

Exercise 2

Write a one-page (250 word) description of what can happen if you drive a car without your license. Be clear and concise

Please use the following words in your letter:
- Feedback
- Objections
- Outcome

HOW TO WRITE INTERNET ARTICLES THAT WILL ATTRACT CLIENTS

Start off with an opening sentence that grabs the reader's attention.

For example:
Last year, I worked on the expansion of Terminal _____ at LaGuardia.

Be specific. Don't let anyone think you worked on the entire airport.

Be specific:
I worked on the runway expansion_____.

I worked on the newly-designed passenger waiting area of Terminal _____.

I worked with my team to upgrade the baggage handling area of Terminal _____.

Building Client Attraction

- Writing an article on a topic related to your product/service will help you to become an expert in your field.
- Write one article a week or at least one article each month on your website.
- Send your articles to organizations that can help you to promote your business.
- PLEASE DO start a mailing list BUT always ask permission to add people to it.
- Your articles should be sent to other authors in your industry who might mention you on their websites. Offer to do the same for them.
- Give a small bit of free advice, for instance, a How To piece. Don't go overboard. Just enough to make the reader feel you're open to giving some free advice.
- Always send a thank you note, even in email format, to everyone who gives you advertising.

SAMPLE ARTICLE

HOW NOT TO ATTRACT CLIENTS TO YOUR BUSINESS

by Jane Carpenter

I went to a lecture last night hoping to find out how to write an article for the Internet to attract new business.
Instead, I listened to someone who went on and on and on about his business.

Don't do this:
I always wanted to walk in my father's footsteps. He was the best dentist in the world. He polished patient's teeth like diamonds using

his special mixture. But first, he took X-rays and a family history. Speaking of which, did I tell you I want to walk in my father's footsteps?

I'll be the third generation. I'm more concerned about cleaning and upkeep than with billing.

I hate dentists who are more concerned with handing out flyers of their services than performing them.

IF I HAD THIS PERSON IN FRONT OF ME, I'D NEED TO BE RESTRAINED FROM RAISING MY HAND AND YELLING "STOP!"

Do this:

Hello, Jane Carpenter here to announce the opening of her dental practice. I'll take care of your cleaning, fillings, gum preservation, and more. Please take a look at my website, select your service, and call me for an appointment.

Competition? Of course. I'm not the only dentist in this city, BUT my services are top notch. If you scroll to the bottom of my website, you'll see a list of satisfied customers—of all ages.

So come in and let me have a look.

I guarantee a thorough exam, and, you'll leave with a smile.

PRESENTATIONS

HOW TO WRITE A SPEECH

Research your topic to see what information is available.

Write an outline that includes the following:

- A brief introduction about yourself
- The facts
- Close by asking if there are any questions

NO JOKES and I mean <u>no</u> jokes. This isn't the comedy hour. Stick to the facts.

If you have authored a book that is germane to the topic, please <u>DO NOT</u> distribute it unless your employer has given you permission. Your job is more important than the proceeds of your book. If your employer says it is all right, you can mention the book at the end of your handout under "Resources." However, if you're in your own enterprise, go for it.

TIPS

- Some speakers prefer to jot down their notes on index cards, which is less cumbersome than a notepad.

- At the end of your talk, jot down the questions that you didn't have time to answer and send replies to the respective attendees.

- Always ask for a list of attendees. This is important to retain present clients if you are employed by a company and crucial if you plan to go out on your own. It could form the foundation of a mailing list.

- Staple your business card to a handout with a brief summary of key points of your talk.

A WORD ABOUT BUSINESS CARDS: NAME, TITLE, EMAIL, AND PHONE NUMBER. KEEP IT SIMPLE. IMPRESS PEOPLE WITH YOUR TALK, NOT YOUR CARD.

HOW TO GIVE A PRESENTATION: VERBAL AND POSTURE TIPS

When you walk up to a podium to give a speech, please make sure you haven't had too much wine or liquor for lunch or dinner. Some people can consume a large quantity of either and pass a sobriety test. Others will wobble after one drink. Leave drinks for after your presentation. Make it your reward.

. . .

When you are at the podium, don't hold onto it for dear life. It's a sign of nervousness. Have confidence. Stand up straight, button that jacket (ladies and men), and lift your head as high as it will go. Keep your hands at your side. I've taught elementary school. When I didn't have my student's attention, I told them to <u>Stop, Look, and Listen</u>. When you reach the podium, especially if you are the first speaker of the day, wait until you have everyone's attention to talk.

Practice your speech in front of a mirror and then record it. Play it back. If your voice wobbles, CALM IT DOWN by meditating for a few minutes before you go live. If speaking in front of an audience is new to you, then choose one person in the audience and focus on them while speaking. Every so often, look to your left and right so the rest of the audience doesn't feel left out. If English isn't your native language, practice your speech the night before in front of a friend. Give them a copy of your speech and tell them to circle any words that you didn't pronounce correctly. You never get a second chance to make a good first impression. Speaking of time, once you find out how long you have to speak, don't run over. Use a kitchen timer or have a colleague time you. Make an outline of what you plan to say. You don't need to bring the entire speech. Write down notes on index cards. You can elaborate in person. Speaking of speed: Moderate your speech. Don't talk too slow or too fast.

NEVER: Scratch your shoulders, play with your hair—for ladies, twirl pens, twist your watch, gnaw on your glasses, or yawn. Make your speech so fascinating your audience won't have the chance to be bored with you. <u>Again, don't make jokes. Leave humor out of your presentation</u>.

Chapter Five
COMMUNICATION

HOW LISTENING SKILLS CAN HELP YOU ACHIEVE YOUR GOALS

Get a New Job or Promotion

You need to listen to what the hiring manager wants to know about you and what you can contribute to the company and its clients. Write down your answers on index cards, practice in front of a mirror, and answer in clear, concise sentences.

Maybe in your last job, you launched an advertising campaign that delivered outstanding results. Before you answer, find out if they want someone results-driven or do they need someone with strong leadership ability? By listening well, you can decide whether your story is about how you led a team through that successful campaign or took the initiative on your own. Use industry terms to show the interviewer that you are familiar with your chosen field.

Increase Productivity

Ask if there is anything specific he/she would like you to focus on.

Innovation and Creativity

Too often we think innovation has to be high-tech or industry-shifting. But creativity doesn't always require Harry Potter magic. Colonel Sanders often slept in his car while he built his empire.

HOW TO DEVELOP TELEPHONE LISTENING SKILLS

Be Polite. Give the listener at the other end of the line your full attention. If you are listening to someone giving a speech, the same holds true. DO NOT check your emails, listen to voice messages, or pour yourself a glass of water. Listen with both ears to what the caller has to say, digest it, and give constructive feedback. NEVER assume you know what they are going to say. <u>DON'T interrupt.</u> You can always contact the caller once you've collected your thoughts.

Don't be afraid to ask questions if there's something you don't understand. Asking questions is part of our process of collecting and understanding information. So asking questions that show you've heard what's been said will help you to give constructive feedback.

Summarize. You'll earn the trust of the caller/colleague/prospective client more easily if you are able to summarize what they've told you.

VOICE MAIL

Please leave a clear, concise message on your cell and home phones. Nothing fancy or long-winded. People are busy. They don't have time to listen to a long message. Be sure to ask for the date and time of their call and ALWAYS ask them to spell their name, spell out the email, and leave a phone number.

As to the recording, don't raise or lower it. Speak in your normal tone. Be pleasant but a bit formal. REMEMBER: The first impression you create is on the phone. Make it a good one.

Chapter Six
ENGLISH AS A SECOND LANGUAGE (ESL) TIPS

CORRECT WORD USAGE

"I always **wash** my face with unscented soap." (A special kind for the face)
"Johnny, wash the floor with that soap detergent." (This is a special cleanser)

"I've always wanted to build a greenhouse." (A house for growing plants)
"I wouldn't want to live in a green house." (The color of a house)

"Be careful with that black magic marker on my yellow jacket." (Garment color)
"I want you to use the yellow highlighter." (For class instruction)

He tried on the brown coat. (Clothing garment)
The house needs another coat of paint. (A painting term)

He brushed each strand of hair. (Refers to pieces of hair on the head) They were stranded at the airport. (Means they had no way to get home)

NEVER SWITCH VERB TENSES

Wrong: I was at home because I am sick.

Correct: I was at home because I was sick.

THAT, WHICH

That

You need "that" to complete the sentence. Otherwise, it won't make sense.

Example: The car with snow tires was the only one that would go up the hill.

Which

If you lifted the information between the commas out of the sentence, it would still make sense.

Example: The blue car, which had snow tires, was the only one that would go up the hill.

Listening Techniques to Learn Correct Word Usage

FOR THIS ONE YOU'LL NEED A TAPE RECORDER OR A COLLEAGUE WHO IS A NATIVE SPEAKER OF ENGLISH

Instructions: Listen to each sentence and repeat it five times. Then pronounce the **boldfaced** word(s) in each one correctly.

There may be signs of human **beings** on other planets.
MAKE SURE TO PRONOUNCE THE "s" IN BEINGS.

Thank goodness I was wearing my seatbelt, or I wouldn't be here.

THERE IS NO SUCH THING AS "THANK**S** GOD OR GOODNESS"

REPEAT THANK GOD 20 TIMES UNTIL THE WORDS ROLL OFF YOUR TONGUE.

He can speak English, but he **pronounces** words with a French **accent**.

Practice is crucial for remembering how to pronounce words in English.

Albert **studied** Korean but can only remember a few words.

Jane forgot to put a **period** inside of quote **marks** and **misspelled** several words in her speech.

Students must **remove** their books from their desks until they finish their **tests**.

The report **concluded** that some people learn English more easily than others.

Learning a language is a challenge that can be **accomplished**.

I try to learn one new **skill** each year.

NUMBERS AND SYLLABLE STRESS

Numbers ending in *–teen* (for example, 14 or 15), sound similar to numbers ending in *–ty* (For example, 50 or 60).

Follow these guidelines:

>STRESS IS ON THE **LAST** SYLLABLE
>14 *four*TEEN
>15 *fif*TEEN

>STRESS IS ON THE **FIRST** SYLLABLE
>FIF*ty* 50
>SIX*ty* 60

NOTING DESCRIPTIONS

To learn new words, write the <u>thing</u> described on the left hand side of a piece of paper.

Then, note the <u>meaning</u> on the right.

Look at the new word and fold it in half, close your eyes, and practice pronouncing it.

Drawing a picture of the object can also help you to remember it.

EXAMPLES

Thing	Meaning
Traffic light	Stop at the red
Lampshade	Used to cover a lamp
Recipe	Used to cook a meal or part of a meal

Chapter Seven
PROMOTING YOUR BUSINESS

MARKETING TECHNIQUES FOR EMERGING BUSINESS OWNERS

Before you look for office space, order letterhead and business cards or find a webmaster to design your website, I want you to think about your product/service.

HOW TO WRITE A SOUND BITE

What is a sound bite?

A message that you can deliver in less than 30 seconds. It's your elevator pitch: A quick description of your product or service that can be described in the time it takes to ride in an elevator. It's the equivalent of writing your description on the back of a business card. Think about the message you want to deliver to prospective clients.

. . .

Appealing, Easy, Convincing

- Appealing enough to attract attention
- Easy enough to remember
- Convincing enough to motivate busy people to contact you

I know what you're thinking: *I'm going to post this on the Internet and magic. Customers will come.* Maybe in the movies—reel life, but not in real life. To succeed, you'll need three things:

Energy, Effort, and Positive Attitude

Energy: We all have this early in the morning, but you'll need enough to carry you through long days and longer nights of getting the word out about your product.

Effort: When the going gets tough, the tough get going and keep on doing.

Positive Attitude: I'm going to succeed.

Content

In your 30 second sound bite, you need to answer the questions:

Who you are—not your whole life history. Only the parts that pertain to your product or service.

What you represent. Please be brief. Give just enough to close the sale.

Why you? Here's where you shine the spotlight on what YOU have to offer.

SAMPLE INTRODUCTIONS

A cookbook author: I'm a graduate of the _____school. I've worked in some of the leading restaurants in _____. My name can be found in the following directories _____.

Construction company: I've built commercial, residential, and retirement properties-on time, within budget. I adhere to building codes, and my record is accident free.

Fitness Coach: I'll make you look good in and out of your clothes. I've worked in top-of-the-line health clubs such as _____.

DELIVERY

1. In front of an audience. Please don't hold onto the podium for dear life. Use it for your notes. Stand up straight. If you're nervous, focus on one person and pretend there is no one else in the room. **Refer to my previous advice.**
2. Attire: A dark suit for men and women is always best. Leave flash for the weekend.
3. Pronunciation: Practice pronouncing names that are challenging.
4. Enunciation: If English isn't your native language, practice difficult words WAY BEFORE you give your presentation **(refer to ESL section)**.
5. When you are done, ask if there are any questions and sit down.
6. Business cards: Always carry a handful in your pocket. For each card you give out, you should get two in return.

MORE ON HOW TO WRITE EFFECTIVE ARTICLES ON THE INTERNET TO PROMOTE YOUR BUSINESS

A. Article Composition

- Select a Topic
- List the Major Points You Want to Cover
- Fill in the Major Points With Key Industry Concepts
- Let the Article Sit for a Week and then Review It
- Write a Realistic Description of Your Work Background
- When It's Ready, Pitch Your Article Idea

B. Advice

Neil Patel has an insightful article on writing that brings in sales. To review it, please go to https://neilpatel.com/blog/write-articles-sell-30-strategic-steps/. The article appeared on Google in July of 2020.

ORGANIZATIONS TO PROMOTE YOUR BUSINESS

Engineering

For all the disciplines—Mechanical, Civil, Geotechnical, Structural, and so on, you need to find your niche. Please use the list on the next page to do the following tasks:

Who do I know? Look through your business cards and start calling colleagues. Do be careful if any of them are still working in your company. Also contact former classmates, professors, and the associations.

DO NOT call former employers unless you're certain they will keep your confidence.

For each association listed, find someone who went to your college/university. Tell them of your plans and ask if they know of classmates who are of a like mind. Again, please do be careful about placing ads in alumni newsletters. News travels fast. It takes time to build up a business. You don't want your current employer to see that you are planning to go out on your own until you have your clients in place.

What do others need to know about you? Join organizations in your discipline, attend conferences, and get on speaking panels. You have to build up your name and brand. Once your peers hear you speak on several occasions (and, yes, travel might be involved), you will become a known quantity. You WANT peers to come to you for industry advice. Build trust, follow through on all inquiries, and they will keep coming back to you.

Mailing lists—Sign up for all mailings that pertain to your discipline. Attend online and in-person meetings. Please don't feel you have to join every association. If your heart isn't in it, your feelings will show on your face. Only attend meetings of organizations where you know you can network effectively.

DO NOT BE A NAME DROPPER

When you attend an event, don't talk about being on great terms with the president and chairman. Make your success happen with your abilities. Use your education and work experience as a springboard to success. Each of us is unique and brings something of value. Your task is to find out where you fit in the industry. *Only perseverance can do that for you.*

Engineering Organizations

AABC Commissioning Group
Accreditation Board for Engineering and Technology, Inc.
Advanced Technology International

Aerospace Industries Association of America (AIA)
American Academy of Environmental Engineers & Scientists
American Association of Engineering Societies
American Indian Science and Engineering Society
American Institute of Aeronautics and Astronautics
American Institute of Chemical Engineers
American Nuclear Society
American Railway Engineering Maintenance-of-Way Association
American Society for Engineering Education
American Society of Agricultural & Biological Engineers
American Society of Civil Engineers
American Society of Heating, Refrigerating and Air-Conditioning Engineers
American Society of Mechanical Engineers
American Society of Naval Engineers
American Society for Nondestructive Testing
American Society of Plumbing Engineers
American Society of Safety Engineers
ASM International
Associated Air Balance Council
Association for Computing Technology
Association for Women in Science (AWIS)
Association of Chinese-American Scientists and Engineers (ACSE)
Audio Engineering Society
Biotechnology Industry Association (BIO)
CAPS Research
Control System Integrators Association (CSIA)
Energy Management Association
Engineering Society of Buffalo
Hardwood Plywood & Veneer Association
Institute for Public Procurement (NIGP)
Institute of Industrial and Systems Engineers
Institute of Electric and Electronics Engineers (IEEE)
Institute of Transportation Engineers
International Society for Optical Engineering (SPIE)
Lightning Protection Institute(LPI)

Manufacture Alabama (MA)
National Council of Structural Engineers Associations
National Society of Black Engineers
National Technical Association (NTI)
North American Society for Trenchless Technology (NASTT)
Order Of The Engineer
Plumbing-Heating-Cooling Contractors-National Association (PHCC)
Refrigeration Service Engineers Society (RSES)
SAE International
Society for the Advancement of Material and Process Engineering
Society of Hispanic Professional Engineers
Society of Manufacturing Engineers
Society of Naval Architects and Marine Engineers
Society of Petroleum Engineers
Society of Plastic Engineers (SPE)
Society of Women Engineers (SWE)
The Society of Tribologists and Lubrication Engineers (STLE)
Tooling, Manufacturing & Technologies Association (TMTA)
Women in Technology (WIT)
Wood Component Manufacturers Association (WCMA)
Wood Machinery Manufacturers of America (WMMA)
Woodworking Machinery Industry Association (WMIA)

Engineering Professional Organizations

American Academy of Environmental Engineers and Scientists (AAEES) serves the environmental engineering and environmental science professions.

American Association for Aerosol Research (AAAR) is a professional organization for scientists and engineers in the field of aerosol research.

American Institute of Chemical Engineers (AIChE) is the world's leading organization for chemical engineering professionals.

American Society for Precision Engineering (ASPE) is a global community advancing the science and art of precision engineering.

American Society of Civil Engineers (ASCE) is the nation's oldest engineering society with 150,000 plus members.

American Society of Heating, Refrigerating, and Air-Conditioning Engineers (ASHRAE) is a global society advancing human well-being through sustainable technology for the built environment.

American Society of Mechanical Engineers (ASME) promotes the art, science, & practice of multidisciplinary engineering around the globe.

Association for Facilities Engineering (AFE) is the oldest and most experienced Facilities Maintenance & Engineering organization in the world.

Association of Energy Engineers (AEE) is a nonprofit professional society of over 16,000 members in 90 countries.

Association of Technology, Management, and Applied Engineering (ATMAE) is a membership organization for educators and industry professionals involved in integrating technology, leadership, and design.

Biomedical Engineering Society (BMES) is the professional society for biomedical engineering and bioengineering.

Illuminating Engineering Society (IES) is the recognized technical authority on illumination.

Institute of Electrical and Electronic Engineers (IEEE) is the world's largest professional association advancing innovation and technological excellence for the benefit of humanity.

Institute of Packaging Professionals (IPP) is committed to leadership in packaging through the continuing education and growth of its members.

International Council on Systems Engineering (ICSE) is an organization formed to share and promote the best principles and practices of systems engineering.

National Association of Power Engineers (NAPE) is the oldest association dedicated to education and training for responsible engineering practices.

National Association of Rocketry (NAR) is the oldest and largest space modeling organization in the world.

National Society of Professional Engineers (NSPE) serves as the recognized advocate of licensed Professional Engineers.

Society of American Value Engineers (SAVE) promotes, advocates, certifies, and educates engineers related to the 'value methodology' and its practitioners.

Society of Petroleum Engineers (SPE) promotes the exchange of technical knowledge within the upstream oil and gas industry.

Society of Petroleum Evaluation Engineers (SPEE) is dedicated to the advancement of the profession of petroleum evaluation engineering.

Society of Plastics Engineers' (SPE) mission is to promote and provide the knowledge and education of plastics and polymers worldwide.

Occupational Safety & Health

American Industrial Hygiene Association (AIHA) is one of the largest international associations serving the needs of industrial hygienists and OEHS professionals.

American Society of Safety Engineers (ASSE) sets the standard for OSH excellence and ethics while providing professional development, advocacy, and standards development.

National Association of Safety Professionals (NASP) provides training, consultative services, and third-party certifications in the area of workplace safety.

Construction Professional Associations & Organizations

Accessibility Professionals Association (APA) is an association of professionals focusing on accessibility in the built environment.

American Concrete Institute (ACI) is a membership organization for individuals involved in concrete design, construction, materials, and repair.

American Welding Society (AWS) advances the science, technology, and application of welding and allied joining and cutting processes worldwide including brazing, soldering, and thermal spraying.

Associated Builders and Contractors (ABC) is a national construction industry trade association representing nearly 21,000 chapter members.

Construction Financial Management Association (CFMA) is dedicated to serving the construction financial professional.

Construction Management Association of America (CMAA) is dedicated exclusively to the interests of professional construction and program management.

Golf Course Builders Association of America (GCBAA) is dedicated to advancing and continuously improving the profession of golf course construction.

Modular Building Institute (MBI) offers membership opportunities for people with an interest in the commercial modular construction industry in both the public and private sectors.

National Association of Construction Auditors (NACA) is dedicated to enhancing the control environment related to construction projects.

National Association of Home Builders (NAHB) is the leading trade association representing the housing industry.

National Electrical Contractors Association (NECA) for electrical contractors performing construction in the design, installation, and maintenance of electrical systems.

National Institute of Building Sciences (NIBS) brings together representatives of government, industry, labor and consumer interests, and regulatory agencies.

North American Die Casting Association (NADCA) represents the die casting industry, more than 3,100 individual members in the U.S., Mexico, and Canada.

IT Professional Associations & Organizations

Agile Alliance is a nonprofit member organization dedicated to promoting the concepts of agile software development.

ASIS International is the leading organization for security professionals worldwide.

Association for Computing Machinery (ACM) is a global community of computing professionals and students with nearly 100,000 members.

Association of Computer Engineers and Technicians (ACE – ACET) promotes professional standards within the IT industry.

Association of Independent Information Professionals (AIIP) is the premier industry association for information professionals working independently.

Association of Information Technology Professionals (AITP) is the leading worldwide society of information technology business professionals.

Association of Software Professionals (ASP) is a professional trade association of software developers who are creating and marketing leading-edge applications.

BICSI is a professional association advancing the information and communications technology (ICT) community.

Computer & Communications Industry Association (CCIA) is dedicated to innovation and enhancing society's access to information and communications.

Computing Technology Industry Association (CompTIA) is the voice of the world's information technology (IT) industry.

EDUCAUSE is a nonprofit association and the foremost community of IT leaders and professionals committed to advancing higher education.

Geospatial Information & Technology Association (GITA) is a professional association and leading advocate for anyone using geospatial technology.

Healthcare Information Management Systems Society (HIMSS) is a global advisor and thought leader supporting the transformation of health through the application of IT.

IEEE Computer Society is the computing professional's single, unmatched source for technology information, inspiration, and collaboration.

Information Systems Audit and Control Association (ISACA) is a global association of IT and cybersecurity professionals.

Information Systems Security Association (ISSA) is a not-for-profit, international organization of information security professionals and practitioners.

International Association of IT Asset Managers (IAITAM) serves in-house practitioners, vendors, and consultants globally.

International Association of Privacy Professionals (IAPP) is the largest and most comprehensive global information privacy community and resource.

International Web Association (IWA) is the industry's recognized leader in providing educational and certification standards for web professionals.

Network Professional Association (NPA) is the leading organization for network computing professionals.

Technology Services Industry Association (TSIA) is the leading professional association of the technology services industry.

User Experience Professionals Association (UXPA) supports those who research, design, and evaluate the user experience of products and services.

Waste Management

Air & Waste Management Association (AWMA) improves environmental knowledge and decisions by providing a neutral forum for exchanging information.

Solid Waste Association of North America (SWANA) is an organization of 9,000 plus public and private sector professionals committed to advancing from solid waste management to resource management.

More Networking Associations

Engineering Exchange - 11,000 engineers around the world discussing various topics in a forum specifically designed for engineers.

CR4 - another forum built specifically for engineers to engage in discussion with each other.

Labroots - a networking and collaboration site for scientists, engineers, and technical professionals.

Element 14 - caters to design engineering professionals.

Chapter Eight
WRITING RESOURCES

The Elements of Style by William Strunk, Jr. and E.B. White –latest edition

The Chicago Guide to Grammar, Usage, and Punctuation by Bryan A. Garner

A Thesaurus for antonyms and synonyms

Webster's Dictionary—most recent edition

A bilingual dictionary for your native language-always helps

WRAP UP

I've given you the "tools" of the trade. Now, proceed with my blessings.

Should you run into a snag, please don't sit in frustration. Contact me: writerjr1044@gmail.com

I'm available for one-on-one consultations or group workshops.

ACKNOWLEDGMENTS

I would like to acknowledge wonderful colleagues, Kelly, PE; Gerri and Dino, and Steven M. who have been my brilliant beta readers in the writing of this handbook. A round of applause to each of you. I would also like to thank my "pro" formatter, Maggie Lynch.

ABOUT THE AUTHOR

Joan lives in the New York metropolitan area, is a published photojournalist, has several short suspense stories online, numerous nonfiction articles on business writing, and taught English as a Second Language to students around the globe. She has three Masters of Science in Medical, Technical, Financial, and Business Writing/Journalism; English as a Second Language, and Special Education.

These degrees fortified by 25 years of corporate and government media writing have taken her on photojournalism and creative writing workshops to Vietnam, South Korea, Hong Kong, South Africa, and Tokyo, Japan. She has also published three nonfiction books on leadership, student motivation, and Autism and is crafting a historical suspense set in World War II.

Currently, she conducts workshops on various aspects of creative and business writing. She has published on a wide variety of topics from cochlear implants to the economy and has conducted workshops-domestic and foreign-on the nuances of business communications for managers and startup companies-all levels.

facebook.com/joan.ramirez.98031
linkedin.com/in/joanramirez1044